How did a fanatical cyclist, ama
son of a piano-tuner marry the
how did they cope with the ten
ambitions to be a writer? Those
along with providing a solution
Enigma Variations.

Hereford Times

When Alice Roberts, daughter of a major-general, married her piano teacher, her family was horrified to be linked to a tradesman. That was one reason for the underlying tension in the marriage of Sir Edward and Lady Elgar. Others explored in this absorbing new play include his refusal to set her poetry to music and, most notoriously, his relationships with other women. Sutton does a skilful job of weaving historic information, and Elgar's reflections on his art, into a plausible picture of the Elgars at home.

Birmingham Post

Sir Edward Elgar is one moment playful, the next cantankerous. He is as unapproachable as he is engaging. As the tensions between Elgar and Lady Alice surface, so do the insights into their marriage. He disregards Alice's poetry, treats her, at times, like a child and it's upsetting to watch. He repeatedly tells her she doesn't understand him, never has and never will, and it's heartbreaking.

Worcester News

Very neat. It's neatly done, altogether. Sutton's text, equally neat, builds in Elgar's searing awareness of his humble origin and self-made stature...and her unthinking snobbery. More fundamental is her pride in her poems, which she longs for him to recognise. Alice's hurt at being a second-best amanuensis flares into jealousy of his succession of friends-patrons-muses.

Oxford Times

Elgar and Alice was first performed at the Swan Theatre, Worcester, on 5th June 2007, before touring to other places associated with Elgar: Hampstead, West Sussex, Harrogate, Oxford and Hereford.

The play was written to mark the 150th anniversary of Elgar's birth on 2nd June 1857.

The cast was as follows:

Sir Edward Elgar	Gerald Harper
Lady Alice Elgar	Janet Hargreaves
Sarah Allen	Katrina Norbury
Lady Alice Stuart of Wortley (Windflower)	Joy McBrinn

The play was directed by Gene David Kirk.

Set design was by Rich Evans.

The text of the play has been revised for publication.

About the author

Peter Sutton has lived on the Malvern Hills for fifteen years, where he has inevitably developed a love of Elgar's music and a curiosity about the composer's complex character.

Peter's comedy *Mr Punch* was shortlisted for the 2005 King's Cross New Writing Award, and his play *My Son Will* was premiered at the 2006 Yerevan International Shakespeare Festival.

As a mature student, Peter trained to act at Birmingham Theatre School, and he has appeared for the European Theatre Company, the Pascal Theatre Company, the Steam Industry and others. He has worked for RADA and the Central School of Speech and Drama, and he has played character parts on television and in short films.

For over twenty years he has been a translator, editor and writer for UNESCO, the OECD, the Council of Europe and other international organisations, and he has published widely in English and German on languages and education.

To Wendy: Gerald Harper

Peter Sutton

ELGAR AND ALICE

To Wendy

With very best wishes

Peter

Severnpix
publishing

First published by Severnpix Publishing
Dovecote Barn, The White House
Suckley, Worcester WR6 5DF

16th June 2008

www.severnpix.co.uk

Printed by Severnprint Limited
Ashville Industrial Estate, Bristol Road
Gloucester GL2 5EU

Mixed Sources
Product group from well-managed forests and other controlled sources
www.fsc.org Cert no. TT-COC-1977
FSC

Designed by Paddy Gormley

A CIP record for this book is available from the British Library.

ISBN 978-0-9545402-4-1

Contents

Photographs

Front cover: Gerald Harper as Elgar, June 2007

Back cover: Gerald Harper as Elgar, Katrina Norbury as Sarah (back row); Janet Hargreaves as Alice Elgar (front left) and Joy McBrinn as Windflower (front right)

The Elgar Marriage

Peter Sutton

Edward Elgar was the son of a piano-tuner who ran a music shop in Worcester, played in an amateur orchestra and was organist at the Catholic church. Edward's mother, the sincere Roman Catholic in the family, had an interest in poetry and encouraged Edward to read books left in store above the shop. All seven children played instruments, and his brother Joe seemed more musically gifted than Edward.

This was the background of plain Ted Elgar, celebrated as England's greatest composer, who was self-taught yet wrote over 140 known works. He married the daughter of a major-general, received a whole string of honours and was appointed Master of the King's Musick.

When I was asked to write a play about him by Catherine Moody, a Malvern painter whose father had known Elgar, there was no shortage of sources. Besides her own researches, other published biographies and archives, materials were provided by Katrina Norbury, who is related to the subject of one of the Enigma Variations and lives in a house that Elgar often visited. She and I set up Elgar Productions to produce the play for the Elgar anniversary.

The information about Alice Elgar, née Caroline Alice Roberts, is more limited. She was born in India and brought up in a large country house near Gloucester; one of the servants there was Sarah Allen, who subsequently joined the Elgar household. Alice's father died when she was eleven, and she and her mother and brothers led a conventional life, supporting the church and the community, and dabbling in the arts. Through friends she developed an interest in geology, compiling the index for a book on the subject. When she was 25 she wrote an essay on the local landscape, and nine years later she became a published novelist. By then she was regularly composing short stories and poems, which demonstrate skill and feeling despite some awkward images and archaisms.

She met Edward when she took piano lessons, and defied most of her family by marrying him. It is clear from her diaries that she fell in love and admired him to the end, but was she also relieved to find a husband at the age of 39? Did she come to regret giving up her own faltering career to nourish his genius? Did she resent his desertion of the Catholic faith, to which she converted? And how did she view his dislike of London life, which she adored, and his constant need for friends of both sexes to supplement her support?

Despite his many friendships, Edward was seldom at ease with himself or others. He was a lover of word play and practical jokes, but could be solitary, crass and extremely rude. What was he like when alone with Alice? Their use of private baby-talk suggests a loving intimacy, but did this reflect the true strength of their marriage? And what did he really think of her poems?

His principal muse, his 'Windflower', was Alice Caroline Stuart Wortley (oddly, she and Alice Elgar shared both forenames). She was the daughter of the portrait-painter Sir John Everett Millais, whose family already had one social scandal in the cupboard: Millais had fallen in love with the wife of the aesthete John Ruskin, and the Ruskins' marriage was eventually dissolved on grounds of non-consummation. Windflower came to know Elgar through the Sheffield Festival, being the second wife of the local Conservative MP, himself an amateur musician. However, while the bulk of Elgar's letters to her are published, some are missing, and hers have almost all disappeared.

Behind Elgar's public persona there was therefore the potential for a play about the tensions of a long-term relationship. As for his music, insights developed as the writing progressed, culminating in the description of his method of composition given in Act I, and in the solution to the 'Enigma' behind the Variations proposed in Act II. Perhaps these come close to the truth, for the play was warmly received by eminent musicians such as Sir Charles Mackerras and by members of the Elgar family.

Taking Elgar and Alice on the Road

Gene David Kirk

I was delighted to be asked to direct the premiere of this play, and I am delighted now that the text will be available to everyone interested in this fascinating subject and its engaging dramatic representation.

For many years I had been a visitor to Malvern, with its magnificent hills and its long tradition as a centre for the arts, and I was one of the very many appreciative listeners to Elgar's wonderful music, but I knew little about the man. Peter Sutton's script abruptly exposed to me a rich seam of insight, emotion and domestic tension. By setting the drama in the declining years of Edward and his wife, Peter has been able to exemplify the family and friendships of a celebrated early twentieth-century citizen, uncovering the anguish within Elgar's marriage and suggesting a flavour of his uncomfortable dalliances with the opposite sex. The Second Act uses a formidable theatrical device to peel away layers of misunderstanding between two hurting people who have persevered with an unsatisfactory relationship.

The creation of the play was a novel element in the portfolio of events designed to celebrate 150 years since the birth of Edward. It was never an easy option. How much more comfortable and comforting to simply perform the man's music. Peter Sutton had immersed himself in the biography of the composer and had realised that Elgar, like many contemporary celebrities, did not enjoy a charmed life on the crest of a wave. Away from the concert hall applause and the pomp and circumstance of regal appreciation, the artist agonised over his successes and failures.

This territory provided me and the cast with rich material to investigate and platform. We were going to reveal warts and all; to communicate what fuelled the man and what frustrated him and those around him as he reached old age.

Elgar was a private man from a relatively humble background. His music struck a chord – to put it mildly – with concert audiences across the country. He developed a public persona as a country gentleman, but he could never quite fulfil this role convincingly because of the weighty baggage of his own family life and his religious upbringing.

Both Gerald Harper and I independently undertook considerable research and sought to absorb the music in its chronological order of composition. These efforts dovetailed in rehearsals and caused us to re-phrase some lines in the text. Ultimately, as Gerald nurtured a sense of the composer and his circumstances, the actor instinctively relished many passages in the play but also sought amendments. Gerald did not think Elgar would say this or that. And I am pleased to report that Peter almost always saw the virtue in the suggested change.

We worked on the script at Gerald's home in Notting Hill, then went into rehearsals at the well-known Drill Hall near RADA. I was always trying to anticipate how the play would work in very different venues. I think I successfully addressed the mechanical challenges but I had not perceived how the production would evolve in hugely different spaces, from the proscenium-arched Swan Theatre in Worcester to the intimate setting of the New End, where our broad-backed stage play became a handsome chamber piece.

Like many others, I was irritated when the Royal Mint decided to remove the image of Elgar from its £20 banknote in the great man's 150th birthday anniversary year. I am proud to have brought to life Peter Sutton's brave, moving and sinewy script, and I am extremely pleased to know that the play script will exist in perpetuity, alongside Elgar's music, for everyone to examine, evaluate and enjoy.

Becoming Elgar

Gerald Harper

Preparing for and playing the role of Edward Elgar has been one of the most satisfying professional experiences for me in recent years. I almost didn't do it, but became so glad I did.

I only take on a couple of projects a year these days. I find I can quite happily spend great amounts of time in Spain, with my family and fishing. But I am constantly asked to consider undertaking plays old and new.

There has to be something very special about a manuscript and a production to persuade me to get back in the saddle. Mercifully my agent is sharply aware of what I might realistically consider and so sifts down the prospects to tolerable proportions.

He posted Peter Sutton's script to me in Spain. I take the reading of a new play very seriously, avoiding all distractions. This includes switching off the telephone. In a darkened room I sat and worked my way through the text. And I didn't think it worked. The author seemed to have taken a scattergun approach to a variety of elements: the man, his music, his marriage, his life, his relationships with other women.

I reached the end and decided this would not encourage me back on the road in an untried touring production. I walked out into the bright sun enveloping my Spanish home and realised that my eyes were damp. Something in Sutton's script had moved me, touched my heart. So I went back indoors and read it again.

No, it didn't work. I did not want to be a guinea pig in a theatrical experiment. And yet the subject matter, the emotions of our great British composer in his latter days, was intriguing, electrifying.

Peter rang me and argued a compelling case about my capacity to fill the great man's shoes. I diplomatically explained a selection of my reservations.

Many writers are painfully precious about their scripts, treating any criticism as a stab in the heart, but Peter sounded prepared to listen and amend, to re-draft and re-structure as necessary. He indicated he would make it work for me, which he believed would make it work for everyone.

This was beguiling, so I agreed to take part.

A few weeks later in Notting Hill I met with Peter and Gene David Kirk and we worked through the text line by line. We analysed what the play was essentially about. Conclusion: a marriage, in which one party has had a monkey on his back – of genius.

Elgar was a man whose presence in a room did not necessarily indicate he was there. Because his mind could be somewhere else entirely, absorbed with plucking images and phrases from trees, noises, landscapes which he could uniquely turn into passages of music that would resonate with audiences one hundred years and more hence. Someone with such capacity is patently going to be hard to live with.

Peter scribbled furiously, nodding in recognition that certain sequences in his existing draft did not sufficiently fulfil the potential for a satisfactory narrative arc. I feared I might have destroyed his enthusiasm, but a month later I received a new version of the play which dealt succinctly, cleverly and theatrically with all the issues that had concerned me.

I hadn't suggested a single line of dialogue, but I was now reading a manuscript that powerfully advanced the story of the key characters and their troubled lives. Peter had come back with a good play. I had been something of a rude midwife.

I know that for many people the exposure of an unhappy marriage is the emotive core of their appreciation of the play. For me two other matters within the manuscript frequently brought a lump to my throat.

Firstly, Elgar's sense of determination to pursue his goals in the face of family indifference or downright hostility. As a young man I remember my father, a stockbroker, considered I was being terribly stupid when I announced I wished to become an actor. To confirm his perception of my proposed foolishness, a string of sour NCOs in the army scoffed at me when I revealed my plans upon casting aside my uniform. Despite these wise heads warning me against the pursuit of my youthful dreams, I persevered, and I'd like to think it's worked out quite well so far.

One particular passage in Peter's play caused me to sob in rehearsals, which in turn strongly informed my performance. In Act Two Edward admits to his wife that he has lost the ability to pluck tunes from the air. He had wept at his failure to find stimulus from his imagination. He knew he had lost those powers that had made him at times a genius.

I had the enormous pleasure and privilege of being a very great friend and close colleague of a knighted British actor. This man had genius, which I and many others witnessed in the early years of his long career. At that time his private life was a shambles. Under the proscenium arch those personal troubles injected his acting capacity with a magical ingredient. I was one of the few who realised how troubled his life was in the wings. Later, when the great man's private life became, mercifully for him, more measured, satisfactory, steady, his stage presence declined marginally, perhaps imperceptibly. He remained one of the most impressive actors of his generation, but he no longer carried the distorting burden of genius on his back.

Peter Sutton's script explores the repercussions of the genius of a great man who has uplifted the hearts of a nation. I was immensely pleased to undertake a happy period of rehearsals, then stick on that massive moustache and commence the tour. And I recognised immediately that the play was very successful with all the audiences fortunate enough to see the premiere production. It was a joy to do, and meant a great deal to me.

Undoubtedly the play is worth reading for its own sake. I'm extremely glad it will be available in print for everyone to appreciate.

ELGAR AND ALICE

Characters

Sir Edward Elgar, aged 62

Lady Alice Elgar, aged 71

Lady Alice Stuart of Wortley* (Windflower), aged 58

Sarah Allen, aged about 65

* The family name Stuart Wortley was changed to Stuart of Wortley when her husband received a peerage.

Pre-performance music: Mazurka from Elgar's Three Characteristic Pieces, Opus 10 No. 1

ACT I

The drawing room of Severn House, Hampstead, the Elgars' home. The date is 29th March 1920. ALICE is sitting in a chair, coughing and ill, idly reading a thick book. EDWARD is working at his papers. There is silence for a while.

EDWARD: Damn.

ALICE: Edward!

EDWARD: Where's that notebook?

ALICE: Which notebook?

EDWARD: The one I've lost, Chicky.

ALICE: What does it look like?

EDWARD: Like they usually do: blue. Or green.

ALICE: You didn't leave it in Brinkwells?

EDWARD: No, I didn't leave it in Brinkwells. I had it here. You don't think something's happened to her?

ALICE: You know she's always late. Put the record back on while we're waiting.

EDWARD: Do you really want to listen to that circus music again?

ALICE: Yes, Eddoo. I do.

EDWARD: Oh, very well.

He puts a record on the gramophone of 'Land of Hope and Glory' from Pomp and Circumstance March No. 1.

(listening critically) No. No, no, no. Ugh. That's better.

He sings along.

'God who made my high tea,
Make the jelly set.'

(lifting the needle from the record) What a lot of tosh!

ALICE: Everyone adores it, Eddoo.

EDWARD: Then everyone is more of a poltroon than usual.

ALICE: You said it would 'knock 'em flat'. You came in to dinner in a bright red golf blazer with a silly grin all over your face.

EDWARD: It did knock 'em flat. All the way from Flanders to Gallipoli.

ALICE: It's you who chose the words.

EDWARD: No, I didn't. I chose the writer, not the words. It's nearly quarter past!

ALICE: Edward, you know as well as I do it would take wild horses to keep her away. Why don't we have another record instead?

EDWARD: Only if it's real music this time.

ALICE: I'm not up to Johann Sebastopol today.

EDWARD: Nor is the cloth-eared British public. Given the choice between the greatest musical genius who ever lived and Land of Hove and Chorley, you both choose me.

ALICE: Of course we do. You conducted it for King Edward.

EDWARD: I'd have conducted a bus for King Edward. 'Give us a leg up, mister, I'm the son of an organ-grinder.'

ALICE: You're not going to have another fit of the disms, are you?

EDWARD: No. It's just that most people in this septic paradise don't know a march from a Lambeth Walk.

ALICE: George likes Pump and Clump too.

EDWARD: Our present sovereign has about as much musical judgment as a doorpost.

ALICE: Is that why you wouldn't attend his coronation?

EDWARD: I am a man of principles, Alice.

ALICE: Perhaps some day you'll tell me what they are.

EDWARD: All he wanted was a folderol.

ALICE: I'd already bought the hat.

EDWARD: I'd write him an abdication march for nothing. Agh, this is hopeless. I've turned it upside down and back to front, but it's just not going to – . Oh, I hate bloody Hampstead.

ALICE: Why don't you go back to Brinkwells tomorrow?

EDWARD: No, Ducky.

ALICE: You need peace and quiet if you're trying to work.

EDWARD: I'm not, I'm only doodling. I just need those bell chimes.

ALICE: What bell chimes?

EDWARD: The ones in the notebook. Honestly, Ducky, sometimes I don't think you understand me at all.

ALICE: Sometimes I don't think anyone could.

EDWARD: You must remember them. Rising thirds.

ALICE: Where did we hear them?

EDWARD: Garmisch or somewhere.

ALICE: Before the war?

EDWARD: We'd hardly have gone to Germany during the war. Here she is!

ALICE: Who is?

EDWARD: I heard the door-bell.

ALICE: It wasn't Innsbruck, was it?

EDWARD: What wasn't Innsbruck?

ALICE: The bell chimes.

EDWARD: Oh, I don't know. *(looking out)* That's odd. There's no sign of her.

ALICE: Perhaps because you didn't hear the door.

EDWARD: Unless it was Carice.

ALICE: Darling, Carice has a key.

EDWARD: Which she's always forgetting.

ALICE: Like her father.

EDWARD: I don't forget things.

ALICE: What about that letter?

EDWARD: What letter?

ALICE: You see?

EDWARD: Oh, for goodness' sake...

ALICE: After you'd flounced out of the rehearsal.

EDWARD: That was donkey's years ago. *(continuing to work, unsuccessfully)* Oh, this is no – . No!

ALICE: Isn't there some other tune that will fit?

EDWARD: No, there isn't. Any more than you can swap corsets with Alice Stuart.

ALICE: Edward!

EDWARD: We can't find a B flat corset, Modom, but we could do you a fetching F sharp.

SARAH ALLEN enters. Her manner reveals her dislike of WINDFLOWER.

SARAH: It's Lady Alice Stuart, ma'am.

EDWARD: You see! I did hear the bell.

ALICE: Very well, Sarah. Show her in.

SARAH: Yes, ma'am.

SARAH goes off.

ALICE: Not much later than usual.

SARAH shows in LADY ALICE STUART OF WORTLEY (WINDFLOWER), who is fashionably dressed.

SARAH: Lady Alice Stuart of Wortley.

EDWARD: F sharp as I thought. Come in, honey.

WINDFLOWER: Edward! And Alice, my dear!

ALICE: Alice.

WINDFLOWER: I'm sorry I'm so late.

SARAH: I'll see about tea.

SARAH goes off.

WINDFLOWER: Westminster was a heaving mass. If you wanted a cab you practically had to lie down in the road. I just can't think where everyone is going nowadays.

ALICE: How sweet of you to come, Alice, when you're so busy.

WINDFLOWER: I simply had to drop by and see my dearest darling namesake before Charlie and I sneak off to Cornwall.

ALICE: To where the windflowers grow?

WINDFLOWER: Yes, to where the windflowers grow. How clever of you. I must say you're looking quite chirpy today. As bright as a button. Isn't she, Edward?

EDWARD: Mm.

ALICE: One day, Alice, I should like to see your Cornish cottage with its windflowers.

WINDFLOWER: You must both come down when the weather's warmer.

ALICE: Edward says they are very beautiful. Don't you, Edward?

EDWARD: Do I?

ALICE: Frequently. Oh, do sit down.

WINDFLOWER: Thank you.

Pause. EDWARD hums to himself.

Well. Isn't this cosy?

ALICE: How was the play? Edward said it was very good.

WINDFLOWER: It was. It's extraordinary how Mr Shaw can keep an audience enraptured for three hours just by atmosphere and chit-chat.

ALICE: What did Charlie think of it?

WINDFLOWER: Charlie had to cry off.

ALICE: So who else was there?

WINDFLOWER: Just the two of us.

ALICE: Ah.

Pause.

WINDFLOWER: What is darling Carice up to today?

ALICE: She's at a charity meeting.

EDWARD: Is that where our Fishface is?

ALICE: She told you, Edward. And I do wish you wouldn't call our daughter that.

EDWARD: I thought she was out with her gentleman friend.

WINDFLOWER: Has she met someone? How very exciting.

ALICE: If you like animals.

WINDFLOWER looks to EDWARD for an explanation.

EDWARD: He has a farm. In Sussex.

WINDFLOWER: Oh. Well – . Handy for Brinkwells. How's her hospital scheme coming along?

EDWARD: The usual crowd have put up subscriptions.

WINDFLOWER: That's what we're there for, Charlie says. Selflessly to serve. But then he would. He's a politician.

Pause.

It was such a shame about her young man in the war.

EDWARD: It was such a shame about every young man in the war.

ALICE: The greatest shame was the Germans starting it.

EDWARD: Before the war, Al, you were as besotted with the Germans as I was. You applauded Richter till your hands fell off, and you turned plain silly as soon as Jaeger set foot in the room.

ALICE: Oh, Jaeger! Jaeger says this, Jaeger says that. I often wonder why he didn't write the music himself.

EDWARD: He didn't write it because it wasn't his job.

ALICE: You know what they say. Those who can, do, and those who can't, become publishers.

EDWARD: That, Alice, is grossly unfair! Jaeger was one of the few people who listened to my music.

ALICE: I listen.

EDWARD: Yes, but he actually heard what I wrote. I owe my whole career to the Germans.

WINDFLOWER: And one or two other people.

EDWARD: You're absolutely right. Cry God for Alice, England and Saint George!

He begins an imitation of a Schuhplattler dance, stamping, whooping and slapping his thighs, shoes and calves, and singing one of his Bavarian Dances.

'Come and hasten to the dancing,
Merry eyes will soon be glancing,
Ha! my heart upbounds.'

He takes WINDFLOWER by the hands and starts to dance with her.

WINDFLOWER: Oh, my giddy aunt!

EDWARD: 'Come and dance a merry measure,
Quaff the light brown ale, my treasure,
Hark! what joyous sounds.'

WINDFLOWER: To be danced with two left feet, is it?

EDWARD: 'Dance, dance, for rest we disdain...'

ALICE: Edward, do mind the furniture.

EDWARD: 'Turn, twirl, and spin round again...'

ALICE: *(overlapping)* I said, mind the...

EDWARD collides with a small table. It falls and breaks.

EDWARD: Oh, dash!

ALICE: Edward!

EDWARD: Our revels now are ended, it would seem.

ALICE: That was an antique.

EDWARD: Yes, Alice. Sorry, Alice.

WINDFLOWER: My fault.

ALICE: No, no. You're not to blame. It's Saint Vitus here who cannot keep still for more than five minutes. You can't even sit still at a concert. You go prowling around at the back like a tiger in a cage.

EDWARD: If you stand still you perish.

ALICE: If you stand still, you don't knock over the furniture. Really, Edward, you are much too old for such nonsense.

EDWARD: *(to WINDFLOWER)* Music-makers are never too old for nonsense, are we, Alice? We are the dreamers of dreams.

SARAH comes in with the tea tray.

And one can never be too old for tea.

SARAH: Shall I leave it on the – *(seeing the table)* Oh, dear.

EDWARD: *(examining the broken table)* All it needs is a lick of glue.

SARAH: If you say so, sir.

ALICE: Bring it over here, Sarah.

EDWARD: My, oh my. Do I spy scones?

ALICE: Scones are what you asked for.

EDWARD: Did I? That was thoughtful of me.

SARAH: Shall you manage all right like that, Lady Alice?

ALICE: Yes, thank you.

SARAH: If you're quite sure.

ALICE: Don't fuss, Sarah.

SARAH: As you wish, my lady.

SARAH goes off, with another look at the table.

EDWARD: *(having examined the table)* There you are, you see. It'll be as good as new when I've finished with it.

WINDFLOWER: Should I pour?

ALICE: I can reach, thank you, my dear.

EDWARD: *(The table collapses again.)* Almost.

ALICE: Dora Penny danced to your tune as well, didn't she, Edward?

EDWARD: As well as what?

ALICE: As well as Alice.

EDWARD: No, my love. Alice is better. Anyway, I like dance tunes. I used to write dozens of them. Great Scott, do you know what I've found? *(He has picked up a notebook revealed by the falling table.)*

ALICE: The German bell chimes?

EDWARD: No. It's the stuff from the Powick Lunatic Asylum.

ALICE: There's a surprise. Milk or lemon, Alice?

WINDFLOWER: Lemon. Thank you.

EDWARD: Do you know how I wrote my first tunes?

ALICE: It was when you went back to the house where you were born.

EDWARD: No, it wasn't.

ALICE: That's what you've always told everyone.

EDWARD: That's when and where, not how.

WINDFLOWER: I don't see the difference.

EDWARD: Then I'll show you.

ALICE: Do you want tea, Edward?

EDWARD: *(selecting a piece of music manuscript paper and giving it to WINDFLOWER)* Hold that up to the light. Go on, hold it up.

ALICE: Tea, Edward?

EDWARD: What? Not now. What does it remind you of?

WINDFLOWER: Watching an eclipse?

EDWARD: I mean the music.

WINDFLOWER: Mozart?

ALICE: Hardly.

WINDFLOWER: Haydn, then?

EDWARD: Not the composer. The notes. The shape.

WINDFLOWER: They're round.

EDWARD: Yes, and?

WINDFLOWER: They have tails pointing up or down.

EDWARD: And?

WINDFLOWER: They look like golf clubs. Or tadpoles.

EDWARD: What about the whole line?

ALICE: If it's tadpoles it must be a frog march.

EDWARD: Oh, Al!

WINDFLOWER: I thought that was rather clever.

ALICE: So did I.

EDWARD: *(to WINDFLOWER)* Forget the tails.

WINDFLOWER: This is like charades, isn't it?

EDWARD: Concentrate on the tune.

ALICE: May I see?

WINDFLOWER: I used to be good at party games.

EDWARD: Follow my finger.

WINDFLOWER: To the world's end.

EDWARD: A sharp rise, followed by a long sequence of falling steps.

WINDFLOWER: Oh! Like Charlie's career.

EDWARD: And what else besides?

ALICE: Most people's careers.

EDWARD: It's like the hills!

WINDFLOWER: Is it?

ALICE: Let me see.

EDWARD: It's like the Malvern Hills. North Hill, the Sugarloaf, the Worcestershire Beacon, and so on.

WINDFLOWER: You old fraud. Are you saying you copied your music from the shape of the Malvern Hills?

EDWARD: Not in so many words. But I must have had them in my mind, because I took that sheet with me once when I was out walking, and when I held it up to shade my eyes, I noticed that the line of the melody did actually follow the outline of the hills.

ALICE: All music has to go up and down sooner or later.

EDWARD: Yes, my love, but the trick is knowing when.

ALICE: Show me, then.

EDWARD: And after I'd gone on another two or three miles, I held it up again, and do you know what I saw?

WINDFLOWER: The same hills.

EDWARD: Yes, but from a different angle. And they matched the variation on the theme I'd already jotted down.

ALICE: Show me, Edward!

EDWARD: Same notes, same hills. Different shape.

EDWARD passes the sheet to ALICE.

ALICE: At last.

WINDFLOWER: Let me get this straight. You're saying you could stroll up on to Hampstead Heath, look at the London skyline, and write a tune that goes up over Saint Paul's and down via the District Railway?

EDWARD: In theory.

ALICE: What's the bass line underneath?

EDWARD: Underground streams.

ALICE: It doesn't look like it.

EDWARD: Then I probably never finished it.

ALICE: And you've left out Table Hill.

EDWARD: I didn't mean it that literally! There's no jam!

ALICE: Don't shout, Edward.

EDWARD: Sarah!!

ALICE: *(the noise)* Oh!

EDWARD: The point is that music is all around us. All you have to do is write it down.

ALICE: If it were that easy, we'd all be writing music.

EDWARD: It is easy. It's in the air.

WINDFLOWER: Like birdsong?

EDWARD: Yes.

WINDFLOWER: Or the ripple of water?

EDWARD: Yes.

WINDFLOWER: Or the wind in the trees?

EDWARD: Anything. Blasting in a quarry, come to that.

ALICE: No wonder modern music's so ugly.

EDWARD: Music isn't just sounds, Al. It's tone, rhythm and pattern. Colour. If a painter looks about him, he sees pictures. The urchin on the street corner. The train rushing over a bridge. Well, a composer sees pictures too. He doesn't just hear birdsong or plashing water; he sees the flight of the bird, soaring, dipping, wheeling and diving; the translucency of the water; the droplets caught in the sun; the shape of the waves breaking on the shore, their colour, their regularity, every seventh wave higher than the others. Or the lie of the furrows on a hilly field, leading down to a broad, placid, meandering river. And as for trees – *(to WINDFLOWER)* you've only to look out there. Well? What do you see?

WINDFLOWER: *(looking out of the window)* The house opposite.

EDWARD: The whole house?

WINDFLOWER: There are trees in the way.

EDWARD: Ahah!

WINDFLOWER: And shrubs.

EDWARD: Precisely. There's a solid block in the background, and irregular, feathery shapes pushing up in front. Now, what instrument would you call the house?

WINDFLOWER: A double bass. Or a cello.

EDWARD: And?

WINDFLOWER: The shrubs are the violins.

EDWARD: Good. Good, good, good. Now look more closely at the trees.

ALICE: If you do, you won't see the wood.

EDWARD: Al! I adore trees. I worship trees. They sing my music. Unless I sing theirs, I'm never sure which. The sunrises through the trees at Brinkwells are like a Turner painting. It's probably why I take so much pleasure in chopping them down.

WINDFLOWER: Edward, you are perverse.

EDWARD: Life is full of perversities. Chop and plant, chop and plant. The ancient round. Look at the pattern of the leaves. Around the edges especially, where the light catches them.

WINDFLOWER: They're in clusters.

EDWARD: Note clusters?

WINDFLOWER: They could be.

EDWARD: Then all you have to do is let them fall on to the paper. And there's your tune.

WINDFLOWER: With the darker leaves the lower notes, and the lighter ones the higher?

EDWARD: Very probably. What about the clouds? Are they bass clouds or treble clouds?

WINDFLOWER: The white clouds are so high they're sopranos. Oh, and look. There's a little grey mezzo.

SARAH comes in and stands listening.

EDWARD: What else can you see?

WINDFLOWER: There's a man coming up the street, pushing a handcart.

EDWARD: Plodding heavily as he climbs the hill. Plom, plom, plom, plom.

WINDFLOWER: And running freely when he goes back down. Pitta ditta ditta ditta.

EDWARD: Now suppose there's another man coming up.

WINDFLOWER: Plom, plom, plom. Will they collide?

EDWARD: They're bound to. Add another coming down.

WINDFLOWER: Pitta ditta ditta ditta.

EDWARD: And then a man with a porter's trolley crossing the road. And what have you got?

WINDFLOWER: A variation again.

EDWARD: On?

WINDFLOWER: A fugue.

EDWARD: Johann Sebastian, pass the lady your baton. What are you staring at, Sarah?

SARAH: I've never thought of things like that before, sir.

EDWARD: Most people don't.

ALICE: Sarah, we seem to have lost the jam.

SARAH: I'm sure I brought it. Yes, here we are. Sir Edward's favourite.

ALICE: Oh, good.

SARAH: All right now?

ALICE: Quite all right, thank you, Sarah.

SARAH: I'll make sure the kettle's filled.

SARAH goes off.

EDWARD: Well, it wasn't obvious.

ALICE: The little things in life often aren't.

WINDFLOWER: What am I supposed to do once I have my tune?

EDWARD: You play around with it, of course.

WINDFLOWER: Change the key?

EDWARD: Yes. Speed it up, slow it down. Turn it sides to middle. Where's my tea?

ALICE: You said you didn't want any.

EDWARD: *(meaning I didn't say that)* I didn't.

ALICE: *(pouring tea)* I thought all you had to do was pluck tunes out of the air.

EDWARD: That doesn't mean they're any good. Not fresh off the tree.

WINDFLOWER: You need to plump them up a bit.

EDWARD: Exactly. You use the fiddle and bassoon, the trumpet and the tuba. The full palette of the orchestra.

ALICE: I'll buy you a colouring book for your next birthday.

EDWARD: There, my darling, you've hit the nail right on the head. There are dozens of tunes I should have coloured in. I could have turned Pomp and Circus Tents into a symphony if I'd known what I know now.

WINDFLOWER: Why don't you?

EDWARD: Because it's too late! Now I have the paint box, I'm running out of time.

WINDFLOWER: You're a late developer, that's all.

EDWARD: Mozart would have been a late developer if he'd had a father like mine.

ALICE: That, Edward, is a very old record indeed, and rather scratched.

EDWARD: It may be old, and it may be scratched, but it still plays true. I was thirty-three – thirty-three! – by the time that first substantial piece, that overture, was accepted.

ALICE: Thanks to a quiet word from me. *(to WINDFLOWER)* Would you care for a scone, Alice?

WINDFLOWER: Thank you.

EDWARD: If my father had had his way, I'd have been a piano-tuner like him. Round the back if you please, Mr Elgar. Tradesmen's entrance. He never, ever talked to me about music.

WINDFLOWER: My parents talked to me about art till they were blue in the face, but I still can't paint a pillar box.

ALICE: Nor can I.

EDWARD: I had all these tunes, and what did he do? Send me to work for a solicitor! He gave me nothing! He told me nothing! He thought nothing, did nothing, was nothing! I'd have pawned the family silver if Carice had needed lessons that badly.

WINDFLOWER: My father had lessons from the moment he could hold a stick of charcoal. They called him Millie the Midget.

ALICE: That was his name, Alice.

WINDFLOWER: Not Millais, darling. Millie. He was a freak show, so small when they brought him to London he had to stand on a box to reach the easel.

EDWARD: As a result of which he knew what he was doing before he was past it.

WINDFLOWER: He never knew what he was doing. Because until his dying day he did what other people told him. Is that what you'd have wanted, Professor Sir Edward Elgar, Order of Merit and a whole wallful of doctorates?

EDWARD: It's what I've had, never mind what I wanted. I could have been a violinist if I'd had proper lessons.

WINDFLOWER: I thought you were a violinist.

EDWARD: At the back desk of the Worcester Glee Club.

ALICE: What nonsense. You played in Birmingham.

EDWARD: I don't care where I played! What I'm saying is...

ALICE: We know very well what you're saying.

EDWARD: Hm.

Pause.

ALICE: I had to learn my craft by doing, too.

EDWARD: Oh, here we go. Alice in Wonderland.

WINDFLOWER: Edward, don't be unkind.

EDWARD: You had a library, Alice. You had intelligent conversation.

ALICE: You have a library now.

EDWARD: Now, yes. Now. Of course I have a library. And a set of golf clubs, and a choice of morning coats, and a peg at the Athenaeum. But not then. Then I had a pile of cast-off books in the attic and a lot of talk about the price of buttons.

WINDFLOWER: Edward, no one cares tuppence how you learnt. What matters is the music you've written.

EDWARD: Most of which was wasted on cheap twiddles and touralays.

ALICE: My poems were not cheap twiddles and touralays.

EDWARD: Some of them were.

ALICE: Edward!

EDWARD: But you still expected masterpieces.

ALICE: I didn't.

EDWARD: You did. You kept leaving them around the house with little billets-doux. 'Eddoo, here's a scribble-bibble.' 'Here's anuvver for my luvver.' 'Will oo set dis, Pettookins?'

ALICE: There's no need to shout at me. I'm not the one who couldn't keep up.

EDWARD: So you took me in hand, and hey presto! The notes just flowed from my pen.

ALICE: Edward, I do wish sometimes you would use all your brain and not just the musical half.

EDWARD: I don't have another half.

ALICE: I did not 'take you in hand.'

EDWARD: Pass me that book of yours.

ALICE: What now?

WINDFLOWER: Edward, leave her be.

ALICE: My novel has nothing to do with taking you in hand.

EDWARD: Yes, it has. *(taking ALICE's book)* It's about enlightening the peasantry.

ALICE: I never 'enlightened' anyone.

EDWARD: No, thank God, but you tried. *(opening the book just before the middle)* 'Do you not think, Mr So-and-so, that that class of people lead such dull lives?'

ALICE: I was writing about educating people to appreciate the arts. About opening their eyes to the culture that you and I take for granted. I should have thought that you of all people would agree with that, rather than sniping.

ALICE begins to choke.

WINDFLOWER: It's all right, my dear. Here, let me...

ALICE: And however much you exaggerate the modesty of your background to enhance the brilliance of your rise, you did not need enlightening. You merely pretend you did. And sometimes you make a first-rate showing at it. *(spluttering and spilling tea down herself)* Oh, drat.

EDWARD: All right, all right, all right. You're right, as ever. I was born at the top of the tree, like you.

WINDFLOWER: Stop it, Edward.

EDWARD: Port out and starboard home, Pa clanking about with stripes down his trousers...

WINDFLOWER: She's not well.

EDWARD: Tea with all the fizgigs in Gloucestershire...

ALICE: Edward!

EDWARD: What?

ALICE: You are now the first to put on court dress and snap your fingers for the Wolseley.

EDWARD: That is because I'm an enigma.

ALICE: You're a hypocrite, not an enigma. And where do you think you're going?

EDWARD: I am going to put Humpty together again.

EDWARD goes off, carrying the broken table.

ALICE: *(calling after him)* You've said you're an enigma ever since you wrote the Variations. And there's nothing enigmatic about them either. They're what they say they are. Pictures of your friends. You should have stuck to the law. *(to herself)* Not that you have ever stuck at anything.

WINDFLOWER: Should I ring?

ALICE: No. Just let me recover my breath.

WINDFLOWER: Would you like another cup?

ALICE: No, no, I'll just – . 'Enigma Variations' indeed! The only enigma is what all the fuss is about. Sometimes I could – .

WINDFLOWER: I'm sorry he's so het up today.

ALICE: Oh, he's always het up. Thank goodness he can go and take it out on his test tubes and his Bunsen burners.

WINDFLOWER: When Charlie's feeling sore-headed he goes off to the Lords and chants about land reform, or the colonies.

ALICE: Which does about as much good.

WINDFLOWER: While you and I retire to bed with a headache and a soft-centred novel.

ALICE: And cause a lot less bother. Perhaps I will have another cup of tea.

WINDFLOWER: *(pouring tea)* May I ask you something, Alice?

ALICE: As long as it doesn't involve shouting.

WINDFLOWER: You don't regret marrying Edward, do you?

ALICE: My family certainly regretted it. My Aunt Car said, 'That Mr Elgar is most unsuitable.' And Aunt Gertrude merely screwed up her nose and uttered the one word 'Trade!' At first they could not forgive me, but when he was received at court they could not forgive themselves.

WINDFLOWER: And you?

ALICE: No. No, I have no regrets.

WINDFLOWER: What about Edward's people? What did they think?

ALICE: I am not aware that they ever did much thinking.

WINDFLOWER: So you don't know the reason for the cloudburst against his father?

ALICE: I have no idea. All I know about his parents is that his father did arrange music lessons for him.

WINDFLOWER: With whom?

ALICE: You'd have to ask Edward.

WINDFLOWER: I see.

ALICE: My dear, I hardly ever spoke to his family.

WINDFLOWER: They can't have been that unwashed. You said Edward did not need enlightening.

ALICE: No, but there is a difference between educational and social enlightenment. Really, Alice, it would have been far too awkward.

WINDFLOWER: Like dropping in for tea with one's grocer?

ALICE: Worse.

WINDFLOWER: It couldn't be.

ALICE: From one's grocer one could at least expect high-class tea.

WINDFLOWER: Then it's pretty remarkable how it's turned out.

ALICE: It is more than remarkable. It's a miracle.

WINDFLOWER: And all thanks to you and the Germans.

ALICE: And you.

WINDFLOWER: I don't do much.

ALICE: Don't you indeed?

WINDFLOWER: Perhaps a nudge in the right direction now and again.

ALICE: You, my dear, are the guiding star.

ALICE holds out her hand, and WINDFLOWER helps her up.

Thank you.

WINDFLOWER: There, now. Quite steady?

ALICE: As steady as I shall ever be.

WINDFLOWER: I'm sorry if we've worn you out.

ALICE: You haven't. I just want to look out of the window.

WINDFLOWER: To see the singing clouds?

ALICE: To make sure that the sky is still blue and the trees are still green. Or have the two of you painted them some other colour while I wasn't looking?

WINDFLOWER: We'd never do that.

ALICE: You already have, sometimes. Oh look, do you see the small brown dog with the bushy tail? Do you suppose it's a foxtrot?

WINDFLOWER: If you were a sculptor Edward would tell you the veins in the marble were dance tunes.

ALICE: And if you were an actress he would say every line was a melody.

WINDFLOWER: Perhaps it is.

ALICE: Not when you have put up with him for as long as I have.

WINDFLOWER: I've put up with him for a good fifteen years.

ALICE: Every day of the week?

WINDFLOWER: Alice, darling, are you saying that we ought finally to do something?

ALICE: Only if you have any intelligent suggestions. No, I thought not.

WINDFLOWER: I worry about you, you know, Alice.

ALICE: Do you? I never realised.

WINDFLOWER: I worry about your overworked imagination.

ALICE: A writer needs imagination.

WINDFLOWER: Only if she wants to write fiction.

ALICE: Fiction is invariably drawn from life. There are your soprano clouds, you see, streaming towards us like a fleet in full sail. And do you see the ridge of hills in the distance? No, you don't. You are still too busy looking at the imaginary string quartet across the road. If you were to stand over there on the south side of London – just there, where we lived when we were first married – you would see us here in Hampstead a lifetime of ups and downs later, with our feet still planted prosaically on the earthen rim of the basin.

WINDFLOWER: Basin?

ALICE: The London basin. Didn't you know I wrote about geology as well?

WINDFLOWER: No.

ALICE: It's the study of rocks.

WINDFLOWER: I know what it is, darling. I'm surprised, that's all.

ALICE: Why? Because Edward makes me out to be some kind of simpleton? The world beneath our feet has always intrigued me as much as the world of feeling. Perhaps because when I was a girl, I could look out of my window and see a stretch of scenery to rival any in England. Grassy slopes, stands of trees, old timbered farmhouses, smoke from cottages hidden in coppices. And Edward's musical Malverns. But when I looked at them, I didn't see tunes, I saw words. Or rather, they made me want to find the words to describe them concisely, accurately. In those days we valued words. We knew our grammar and our syntax, and we expected our readers to be able to follow what we wrote. Now no one has any stamina, and everything has to be pithy sayings.

WINDFLOWER: I hope you didn't give up words on Edward's account.

ALICE: Have you never noticed that if you give up a small thing, you gain a larger in return?

WINDFLOWER: No.

ALICE: Nor have I. But one artistic genius in the house is more than sufficient.

WINDFLOWER: Charlie says I never give up anything if I can help it.

ALICE: In that case, perhaps you can do something for me.

WINDFLOWER: I can try.

ALICE: Because it might well require some tenacity.

WINDFLOWER: It depends what it is.

ALICE: There are some of my poems on the table.

WINDFLOWER: These?

ALICE: Yes.

WINDFLOWER: And?

ALICE: I should like you to persuade Edward to set more of them.

WINDFLOWER: It would take more than tenacity to do that.

ALICE: I know what he said, but he liked them well enough once. And he still has tunes growing out of his finger-tips, or falling on his head from the sky, or wherever it is they come from.

WINDFLOWER: Which is no doubt what makes him so crotchety.

(picking up sheets from the pile and reading)

WINDFLOWER (cont.):

> 'Come and hasten to the dancing,
> Merry eyes...'

You wrote that Highland Fling thing that Edward had me dancing?

ALICE: A set of six.

WINDFLOWER: Whatever for?

ALICE: Amusement.

WINDFLOWER: Yes, of course. I was only – I thought it was German, that's all.

ALICE: It was, when I wrote it.

WINDFLOWER: Oh. *(taking another sheet)*

> 'Come back, the sea lies still,
> Rests, and forgets its pain...'

That's a bit – different. How many of these did you have published?

ALICE: Most came back with polite rejections.

WINDFLOWER: Some people have no taste.

(another sheet)

> 'Fair breaks the spring o'er copse and mead...'

Oh, crikey.

ALICE: I can't persuade him, so I thought you might try.

WINDFLOWER: I'll do my best.

ALICE: Thank you.

WINDFLOWER: We'll just have to hope he's in a good mood.

ALICE: And I hope you won't be disappointed.

WINDFLOWER: I hope you won't.

ALICE: I meant on your own account.

WINDFLOWER: Why should I be?

ALICE: Once he stopped making use of my poems, he had no further use for me.

WINDFLOWER: Oh, Alice darling, I can't believe that. And in any case, I don't write poems. I play the piano, that's all.

ALICE: Then you had better play as well as Paderewski, or he'll start being rude about you too.

WINDFLOWER: And I listen, and I tell him what he wants to hear.

ALICE: That's what I used to do. But then I started telling him what I thought he ought to hear, and he didn't enjoy it quite so much.

A small explosion and crash of breaking glass are heard offstage.

WINDFLOWER: What was that?

ALICE: I shouldn't worry. It happens all the time.

WINDFLOWER: I'd better go and see.

ALICE: It's probably too much eye of newt.

A clock strikes four.

Goodness, is that the time? Doesn't it pass swiftly between friends?

WINDFLOWER: We are still friends, aren't we?

ALICE: Of course. We always shall be. Which is why you'll look after him, won't you?

WINDFLOWER: Look after him?

ALICE: When I'm gone.

WINDFLOWER: Now you're being morbid.

ALICE: He insists on seven hot water bottles. But I expect you know that already.

WINDFLOWER: How should I know how many...

ALICE: He says he catches chills so easily.

WINDFLOWER: He does, poor lamb.

ALICE: And his eyes have been troubling him.

WINDFLOWER: Alice, honestly – .

WINDFLOWER goes off.

ALICE: Give my love to Charlie, won't you?

ALICE goes to EDWARD's table. She picks up the sheet that he was working on.

(singing a rising phrase: together with the subsequent descending steps it could be the opening of the Empire March of 1924) Da dáá da dáá da dáá dúm. I wonder what that's not going to be. *(picking up a second sheet and singing a series of descending steps)* Páá pa pa pa pa páá púm. Oh, it's the Grand Old Duke of York again. Up one side of the hill and down the other. And nowhere much in between.

(taking up the sheet of notepaper and reading) 'My dearest Rosa, Thank you so much for your note. I am not sure when we can ...' 'My dearest Rosa.' Well, well, Mrs Stuart Wortley. We are not alone.

SARAH comes in.

SARAH: We shall have to tie you down, Lady Alice, if you're going to keep going walkabout without your stick.

ALICE: Am I so dreadfully naughty?

SARAH: They tied me to the bedpost once. When I was small.

ALICE: I don't think I'm ready for that quite yet.

SARAH: Then let me do the cushion. There.

ALICE: Thank you. No obvious cataclysm in Vulcan's forge?

SARAH: No what, ma'am?

ALICE: Sir Edward's laboratory. He's still in one piece?

SARAH: Oh yes, he's cussing and swearing at his test tubes as right as anything.

ALICE: Sarah, what will happen when the thread breaks?

SARAH: We shall count ourselves lucky to have known a loving and gracious lady, and long may our luck continue.

ALICE: And Sir Edward?

SARAH: He will feel just the same.

ALICE: Thank you, Sarah. You are a dear, kind, loyal soul.

SARAH: Someone has to be. Now, are you sure you wouldn't rather lie down?

ALICE: I'm all right for the moment.

SARAH: Then I'll clear these things.

ALICE: *(handing it over)* My cup.

SARAH: *(of WINDFLOWER's half-eaten scone)* Nothing wrong, I hope?

ALICE: No. As delicious as ever.

SARAH: I'll tell Cook. Only she was worried about the mixture, and I know you don't like waste.

ALICE: It is a sad fact of life that those who already have plenty generally take more than they need.

SARAH: Be grateful for what you have, that's what I was taught.

ALICE: Yes, Sarah. But you and I are old-fashioned about such things.

SARAH: And there's no shame in that, my lady.

EDWARD and WINDFLOWER return. EDWARD has a scarf tied over one eye.

EDWARD: A vast behind, me hearties! Be ye shipshape again, my little treasure?

ALICE: I shall soon be buried, if that's what you mean.

EDWARD: Oh, Al!

WINDFLOWER: Darling, really!

EDWARD: I was trying to cheer you up. Shiver me mainbrace, that kind of thing.

ALICE: The joke has worn rather thin.

EDWARD: Since when?

ALICE: The last thirty years.

EDWARD: Oh.

ALICE: What happened this time? The usual broadside?

WINDFLOWER: He lit a match and forgot he'd turned on the gas.

EDWARD: Improve each shining hour, that's what you keep telling me.

ALICE: With composing, not alchemy.

EDWARD: I've made more money out of my sulphuretted hydrogen apparatus than I ever have out of music.

WINDFLOWER: You can't have.

EDWARD: I have by the hours I've spent on each. My patent stinks machine is in every school in Herefordshire. In fact I'm thinking of doing more...

ALICE: Then we had better increase the insurance.

EDWARD: I want to make a study of diatoms, extract ambrosia from sunlight...

WINDFLOWER: You sound like Faust.

EDWARD: Every artist sells his soul sooner or later.

WINDFLOWER: What did you get in exchange for yours?

EDWARD: I was short-changed.

ALICE: Sarah, I think after all I shall lie down.

WINDFLOWER: I'll come and see you before I go.

ALICE: There's no need for that.

WINDFLOWER: I'd like to.

EDWARD: We shan't be long.

ALICE: Be as long as you like. See if you can find a cure for broken hearts.

ALICE and SARAH go off.

Pause.

EDWARD: Did she want me to set more of her poems?

WINDFLOWER: Some of them.

EDWARD: You should have told her poetry is music in itself. That's what I always say.

WINDFLOWER: I wish you were kinder to her, Edward.

EDWARD: I would be if she didn't write like her grandmother.

WINDFLOWER: They can't all be...

(selecting one of ALICE's poems and reading)

'Flow the sails and flies the boat,
Skims the waves as shadow light...'

That one's not so bad.

EDWARD: 'I'll have you know I have been compared to Tennyson.'

WINDFLOWER: Well, there you are, then.

EDWARD: I don't set anyone's poetry any more.

WINDFLOWER: Not even if Tennyson had written it?

EDWARD: I wouldn't set it if God Himself had written it. I've tried to explain, but she can't or she won't understand. All my life, I tell her, I've been struggling to get away from words. From people and places. Yet she still says she wants me to write more songs. Or more Enigma Variations. They're just as bad – a string of ingenious tunes about people closing doors and fishing dogs out of rivers. They don't go anywhere.

WINDFLOWER: Where do you want to go?

EDWARD: Towards some kind of ideal, I suppose.

WINDFLOWER: When I was growing up, the house was full of artists claiming they were working towards an ideal. What most of them meant was, Please may I paint you naked, Miss?

EDWARD: At least with me you keep your clothes on.

WINDFLOWER: I feel stripped naked in the violin concerto.

EDWARD: You're supposed to. And there's a hint of thigh in the second symphony.

WINDFLOWER: Mine or King Edward's?

EDWARD: *(laughing)* He's in there somewhere, the old King-man who was always so kind to me. But the body of the symphony is yours.

WINDFLOWER: As an ideal, or a naked lady?

EDWARD: Both. I've distilled the bare essence of you.

WINDFLOWER: In your laboratory?

EDWARD: In my heart.

WINDFLOWER: Thank you, my little walrus.

EDWARD: You're in the first symphony as well.

WINDFLOWER: I didn't know I had a foot in each.

EDWARD: I've tried to express you as an abstract thought, rather than the way you walk or talk or eat a pork pie.

WINDFLOWER: That's just as well.

EDWARD: Because I'm trying to write pure music, music that requires effort on the part of the listener.

WINDFLOWER: Don't make it too difficult, or no one will understand it.

EDWARD: That's what Alice says. But we all have brains, so why can't we use them?

WINDFLOWER: I've never understood how Alice can be so brainless sometimes.

EDWARD: What did you say?

WINDFLOWER: I said, I've never understood...

EDWARD: That's enough.

WINDFLOWER: It's true. If she thinks she's as good as Tennyson.

EDWARD: It may be true, but I won't have you say it. I won't have you put her down!

WINDFLOWER: You do.

EDWARD: That's different. I'm her husband.

WINDFLOWER: I'm sorry.

Pause.

What did you do with the table?

EDWARD: I'll deal with it some time. When Alice has pestered me enough.

WINDFLOWER: How ill is she really?

EDWARD: Yesterday she could hardly get out of bed at all.

WINDFLOWER: Oh, Edward.

EDWARD: I don't know what to do. I don't know whether to jolly her along, to say how much I'll miss her, to play music to her, or to leave her to it and curl up in the corner and cry.

WINDFLOWER: I wish there were some way I could help.

EDWARD: You do.

WINDFLOWER: How?

EDWARD: By being there. I can't think what will happen when she does slip away.

WINDFLOWER: To you?

EDWARD: To me. To Carice. To everything.

WINDFLOWER: We shall take care of you.

EDWARD: Will you?

WINDFLOWER: All of us will. All your enigmatic friends. And you'll still write your marvellous music, won't you? Edward?

EDWARD: Hm.

WINDFLOWER: Who knows? When you reach out for a tune, maybe it'll be Alice who hands it to you, sitting up there on a cloud, strumming a harp.

EDWARD: She'll probably rap my knuckles with the thing.

Pause.

WINDFLOWER: I'm sorry I was beastly about her.

EDWARD: And I'm sorry I snapped at you.

WINDFLOWER: I'm used to it.

EDWARD: Do you know why I call you my windflower?

WINDFLOWER: Yes, but tell me anyway.

EDWARD: Because you turn your back when the cold wind blows and bow unbroken before the squall.

WINDFLOWER: And I smile when the sun comes out.

EDWARD: And because you're beautiful.

WINDFLOWER: As beautiful as Dora Penny?

EDWARD: How do you know about Dora Penny?

WINDFLOWER: Alice mentioned her.

EDWARD: Alice mentions all sorts of things.

WINDFLOWER: Was Dora one of my predecessors on this wobbly pedestal?

EDWARD: If she was, it was a much shorter pedestal.

WINDFLOWER: Alice said she danced.

EDWARD: She did. And when she'd done with dancing, she'd sit with her hands round her knees and listen. And turn pages without my having to ask. And laugh when I laughed, and be silent when I was silent.

WINDFLOWER: Someone else you should have married.

EDWARD: Oh! She was a child. A breath of woodland air. A sprite.

WINDFLOWER: How many more of your Variations were you in love with?

EDWARD: Well, in one of them, I'll confess I was thinking of two women at once. That's why I wrote the three dots.

WINDFLOWER: Three women called Dot?

EDWARD: Two into three won't go.

WINDFLOWER: As we know.

EDWARD: One was Mary Lygon. That's who Alice thinks it is – but as usual, she's only grasped half the truth. And the other was Helen, who sailed away to the Antipodes.

WINDFLOWER: The face that launched a thousand sharps?

EDWARD: Until she threw me over.

WINDFLOWER: Poor old Edward Bear. Tossed in the corner again.

EDWARD: She was the first woman I was ever truly in love with.

WINDFLOWER: The first is always the worst.

EDWARD: And therefore seldom the best.

WINDFLOWER: Who can you be thinking of?

EDWARD: 'Rarely, rarely comest thou, spirit of delight.'

WINDFLOWER: What are you writing now for your spirit of delight?

EDWARD: Nothing much.

WINDFLOWER: You must be writing something.

EDWARD: Bits and pieces. Tiddly-poms.

WINDFLOWER: May I look?

EDWARD: If you want.

WINDFLOWER picks up the letter to Rosa.

Give that to me.

WINDFLOWER: *(examining one of the sheets of music)* This is like the man with the cart. *(singing the same descending notes as ALICE)* Páá pa pa pa pa páá púm. *(finding the second sheet, with the rising phrase)* And here he is, going back up again. *(singing the rising phrase)* Da dáá da dáá da dáá dúm. You ought to turn it into a march. The Hampstead Huzzah. You could have some fun with it. Shall I play it through?

EDWARD: Not now.

WINDFLOWER: You're not to leave it lying in a corner, Edward.

EDWARD: I shan't.

WINDFLOWER: Because I know you.

EDWARD: Like Alice.

WINDFLOWER: Inspiration, not aspiration, is what I try to give you.

EDWARD: Perhaps I need both.

WINDFLOWER: I wish I could paint. I'd make a mural of all the women in your music.

EDWARD: With yourself at the centre.

WINDFLOWER: You'd be at the centre, with Alice looking over one shoulder and Helen over the other, being jostled by your gaggle of lovelies.

EDWARD: What about you?

WINDFLOWER: I'd put a garland of windflowers round your neck.

EDWARD: I thought of Helen when I was writing the cello concerto.

WINDFLOWER: Why?

EDWARD: It's something I've never told Alice.

WINDFLOWER: There are several things you've never told Alice.

EDWARD: I saw in the casualty lists that her son had been killed.

WINDFLOWER: And you thought of what might have been?

EDWARD: Yes.

WINDFLOWER:

'Farewell the neighing steed and the shrill trump,
The spirit-stirring drum, th'ear-piercing fife,
The royal banner, and all the quality,
Pride, pomp and circumstance of glorious war!'

EDWARD: 'Pride, pomp and circumstance.' You're the only person who's ever understood the irony of that.

WINDFLOWER: I'm the only person who's ever understood you.

EDWARD: Including myself.

WINDFLOWER: Especially yourself. Would you have liked a son?

EDWARD: I love my daughter.

WINDFLOWER: But?

EDWARD: I suppose every man secretly wants a son.

WINDFLOWER: Don't look at me, my little gigolo.

EDWARD: Alice was nearly forty when we married, so we never thought of another child.

WINDFLOWER: What a pity.

EDWARD: Why?

WINDFLOWER: Because you were still a babe in arms.

EDWARD: It's never made that much difference. Most of the time we thought I'd be the one to pop off first.

WINDFLOWER: You, my angel, are what is called a hypochondriac. Unlike Charlie, who has the constitution of an ox, and similar sensitivities.

EDWARD: I am delicate, that's all.

WINDFLOWER: I know you are, my sweet. But a peck on the cheek from me cures anything from gout to galloping consumption.

EDWARD: That's one of the reasons I love you.

WINDFLOWER: The kiss works because you love me.

EDWARD: Yes, bless you.

WINDFLOWER: Would you like me to stay?

EDWARD: No.

WINDFLOWER: I could tell Charlie I won't come to Cornwall.

EDWARD: I shall cope.

WINDFLOWER: And we're supposed to be going to that dinner next week.

EDWARD: You'll have to take your husband for a change.

WINDFLOWER: It's you they want to meet.

EDWARD: Tell them to make do with a record. Does Charlie know?

WINDFLOWER: So do the girls.

EDWARD: I'm sorry.

WINDFLOWER: For them? Or me?

EDWARD: For all of us. If I had not married dear Alice...

WINDFLOWER: You'd have written a lot less music.

EDWARD: And if you had not married honest, dependable...

WINDFLOWER: Upright, adorable...

EDWARD: Soft-hearted old Charles...

WINDFLOWER: You would never have met me.

EDWARD: In which case...

WINDFLOWER: You would only half have lived.

EDWARD: I would only half have loved.

Elgar's violin concerto begins to play (1st movement, from the entry of the violin).

END OF ACT 1

End of interval music: Slow movement of Elgar's 2nd Symphony or the Mazurka from Opus 10 No. 1 again, as at the opening of Act I.

ACT II

ALICE's bedroom at Severn House, a week later: the evening of 7th April. ALICE is in bed, EDWARD at her side. She is sleepy, and barely able to talk.

EDWARD: You've had another sackful of messages. From Mr Boult – that nice young conductor we heard last month – from Beatrice Harrison, who played my cello concerto so splendidly for you, from Henry Wood, from my brother Frank, who says he's quite well again, though he's missing the shop... I can't remember them all, but they all send you their love.

ALICE: *(murmuring indistinctly)* I'm glad Father Valentine came.

EDWARD: Mm? What? Yes, I'm glad Father Valentine came. Everyone could do with forgiveness from time to time. Oh look, do you see the yellow wagtail? I haven't seen one of those for ages. We had a pied flycatcher at Brinkwells last week, did I tell you? There used to be dozens of them, in Malvern.

ALICE: *(indistinctly)* The people at the post office...

EDWARD: The post office? What about the people at the post office?...

ALICE: *(indistinctly)* What were they... (called)?

EDWARD: *(overlapping)*... Don't worry about them. I'll make sure they're included. I wonder what happened to the dove we kept. It laid an egg, now I come to think of it. Rather like me. There it is again. A flash of golden sunlight. Would you like me to prop you up so that you can see? Or I could move the bed nearer the window.

ALICE: *(indistinctly)* And the telegraph boy...

EDWARD: And the telegraph boy.

ALICE: *(indistinctly)* Tom. Is he Tom?

EDWARD: It's all taken care of, Chicky. I've been through the list twice with Carice. A pound each.

ALICE: *(indistinctly)* The porters... John and...

EDWARD: Ten shillings is enough for the porters. Never mind their names. You just concentrate on making them wait for your little remembrances.

SARAH enters carrying a vase of flowers including red roses, and a mug of Bovril.

Oh, look what Sarah's brought. Aren't they beautiful?

SARAH: I'll put them over here, where you can see them.

EDWARD: Your favourite colours: *(as appropriate)* red, yellow...

SARAH: There. Just right with that bit of greenery. And there's a card, sir.

ALICE: *(indistinctly)* You mustn't forget.

EDWARD: *(overlapping, taking the card)* 'To darling Alice, a few flowers from Cornwall. See you soon. With fondest love from – Alice and Charlie.' Isn't that kind of them?

ALICE: *(murmuring indistinctly, becoming agitated)* We must talk to the Rector.

SARAH: Now, don't upset yourself, Lady Alice.

EDWARD: Well, take them away if they're upsetting her.

ALICE: *(indistinctly)* We have to see about tea and so on.

SARAH: *(overlapping)* It's all right, it's all right. Sir Edward and I will see to everything. It's not the flowers that's upsetting her, Sir Edward. She's talking about the arrangements.

EDWARD: Ducky, you must stop worrying about such things. We're going to have you up and about again before you can say The Wand of Youth.

ALICE: *(indistinctly)* Minnie will be doing it if we don't watch out...

SARAH: Oh, I see, it's not the arrangements after all. She will, won't she, my lady?

EDWARD: She will what?

SARAH: Take over the tea tent. There's a cup of hot Bovril for you, Sir Edward.

EDWARD: What tea tent?

SARAH: Minnie at the garden party. She's thinking about when she was a girl. At Hazeldine.

EDWARD: Oh.

ALICE: *(murmuring indistinctly)* Read me a poem, Eddoo...

SARAH: *(the flowers)* They look a real treat, don't they, Lady Alice?

EDWARD: *(reading the card that came with the flowers)* They should be back tonight. For some boring dinner, Alice says...

ALICE: *(murmuring louder)* ...Poem, Eddoo. Poem...

EDWARD: *(overlapping)* ...I suppose that means they might pop in if they have time.

SARAH: She wants another of her poems.

EDWARD: What? Oh. Er –

(picking up a poem.)

'Love the earth a little while,
For shadows swiftly flee...'

SARAH: Sir Edward!

EDWARD: Hm?

SARAH: Not that one.

EDWARD: Ah. *(picking out a different poem)*

'When shall I see the gladdening smile…'?

SARAH nods approval.

'When shall I see the gladdening smile
Which lies on thy too pensive brow…'

Are you listening, Alice? Alice!

SARAH: She's fallen asleep again. That's all.

EDWARD: Are you sure?

SARAH: Quite sure. You can see her breathing, soft and easy. You'd better sit quiet yourself a while, sir.

EDWARD: What about you?

SARAH: Sir Edward, the war may have changed many things, but I have…

EDWARD: Yes, yes. All right, all right.

SARAH: I have known Lady Alice since I was twelve, Sir Edward, and I shall stay right by her till one of us cracks. Now, will you drink that Bovril I've brought you?

EDWARD: Sarah, were you ever a nanny?

SARAH: Some people need nannies when they're little, Sir Edward, and some people need them when they're big.

EDWARD: For the last thirty years my wife has been my nanny.

SARAH: And a jolly good job she's made of it. Drink up while it's hot.

EDWARD: We never truly escape, do we, Sarah?

ALICE: Escape what, Sir Edward?

EDWARD: Childhood. Our parents.

SARAH: I'm not sure I ever wanted to.

EDWARD: Do you know, when they gave me the freedom of Worcester, I doffed my cap as we passed the shop, and there was my father upstairs, peeping out, with tears in his eyes.

SARAH: So I've heard.

EDWARD: And now when I look in the mirror, I see him looking back.

SARAH: We all see our parents looking back in the end, Sir Edward. That's when we start to understand them.

EDWARD: But I walk like him. I talk like him. I pace about muttering to myself like him. I grouch at my wife like him.

SARAH: I've noticed.

EDWARD: And I wish, I wish, unlike him, that he had done something with his life.

SARAH: Then it seems to me that you have escaped, because you've certainly done something with yours. Finished?

EDWARD: *(the Bovril)* Yes. Satisfied?

SARAH: It'll do. Now close your eyes while I look after Lady Alice.

EDWARD: Bring me a pen and paper first.

SARAH: You're not to wear yourself out writing.

EDWARD: Just a short note.

SARAH: *(bringing the pen and paper)* Because I can cope with one of you in and out of bed, but I can't cope with both.

EDWARD: You worry about yourself for a change, Sarah.

SARAH: On no, not me, Sir Edward. I never worry about me. That's what makes people ill.

SARAH goes off. EDWARD starts to write to WINDFLOWER.

EDWARD: 'My dearest Windflower...' I wish you were here.

He goes on writing.

ALICE gets out of bed and comes to his side. In this scene, she never makes physical contact with EDWARD.

It's all right, Sarah. I shan't be long. Alice! What are you doing out of bed, Chicky?

ALICE: I'm feeling better.

EDWARD: Are you? That's wonderful. I told you you'd be up and about again in no time. Is there anything you'd like? Tea? Soup?

ALICE: No, thank you.

EDWARD: Bovril?

ALICE: I shall just sit quietly. Who are you writing to?

EDWARD: The usual piffle. 'Would you please judge our next bagpipe competition?'

ALICE: How often do you write to Rosa?

EDWARD: Rosa?

ALICE: Yes. Your dearest Rosa.

EDWARD: Ducky, Rosa pedalled out of our lives when the school collapsed.

ALICE: But how often do you write to her?

EDWARD: Occasionally.

ALICE: How occasionally?

EDWARD: I write to her when she wants my advice.

ALICE: On what?

EDWARD: On music, of course!

ALICE: Of course.

EDWARD: Al, we owe her a great deal.

ALICE: Such as your little Welsh tune?

EDWARD: Among other things.

ALICE: A jolly souvenir of your holiday.

EDWARD: That wasn't a holiday.

ALICE: Oh?

EDWARD: It was a hectic weekend in the company of enough of her nephews and nieces to start a school of their own. When I wasn't being buried in sand, they were fitting me out with a bathing costume that made me look indecent.

ALICE: You ought to have married her.

EDWARD: I could never have married an intellectual.

ALICE: You don't think you did?

EDWARD: No. And nor did you.

ALICE: Then it was Dorabella.

EDWARD: Are you sure you should be talking, Chicky? We don't want you having a relapse.

ALICE: She was another bicyclist.

EDWARD: Bicycling is vital, Al. It aerates the brain. It provokes new shapes, new forms, new rhythms.

ALICE: New morals.

EDWARD: I went bicycling with hosts of people. The whole of the Malvern Cycling Club, for a start.

ALICE: But not with me.

EDWARD: That is because you never learnt, my sweeting.

ALICE: I tried.

EDWARD: *(remembering the occasion)* Yes. And I'm sorry I laughed.

ALICE: Until she married and moved away.

EDWARD: Al...

ALICE: And you dropped her.

EDWARD: Dora helped with the archives, that's all. She still does.

ALICE: She did not bicycle all the way from Wolverhampton to stick cuttings in an album.

EDWARD: Al, if you're going to list everyone I ever crossed handlebars with, we shall be here all night.

ALICE: I can still hear the two of you laughing as you came back in from the woods.

EDWARD: She found me amusing. Like most people.

ALICE: Like most women.

EDWARD: I swear...

ALICE: I would rather you didn't.

EDWARD: I do swear, by all I hold sacred...

ALICE: Which is not much any more.

EDWARD: That I never deceived you. With Dora. Or with Rosa. Now, may I finish this note?

ALICE: There are two kinds of deception, Edward. One is physical, and the other is emotional. And because the second kind touches our feelings, it hurts all the more.

EDWARD: What do you want me to say?

ALICE: I was never your muse, was I?

EDWARD: I beg your pardon?

ALICE: I said, I was never your muse.

EDWARD: Ducky, you gave me everything.

ALICE: Except inspiration.

EDWARD: You were my strength, my staff, my amanuensis.

ALICE: But Rosa was your muse.

EDWARD: She was a friend.

ALICE: Until it was Dora.

EDWARD: She was a friend too. They were both friends. Yours as well as mine. Look, I'm tired, so why don't we close our eyes for a bit?

ALICE: Along the way there've been other muses, haven't there?

EDWARD: Along the way there have been other friends. If Rosa was my muse, and Dora, then so was everyone from King Edward to Ivory Hatpins.

ALICE: You've never been messing about with shop-girls?

EDWARD: Ivor Atkins, Al. The organist at Worcester. I've had dozens of muses. Men as well as women.

ALICE: And now it's Alice Stuart Wortley.

EDWARD: Alice Stuart Wortley is not my muse! Well, what if she is?

ALICE: Norwich?

EDWARD: Norwich? It's a city. In Norfolk. With a cathedral.

ALICE: And a festival.

EDWARD: Sometimes.

ALICE: Which you have attended.

EDWARD: When I've been invited.

ALICE: With Alice who isn't your muse.

EDWARD: You could have come.

ALICE: I was busy buying this house.

EDWARD: Which I didn't want.

ALICE: To be more precise, the Norwich Mercury, October the twenty-eighth, 1911.

EDWARD: The photographer made a mistake.

ALICE: Perhaps he took a picture of the truth. 'Sir Edward and Lady Elgar.'

EDWARD: We weren't even arm in arm. You can't think...

ALICE: Oh yes, I can.

EDWARD: Oh Al, everybody knows we go to concerts together. To dinners, to plays, to exhibitions. While you're busy buying houses and Charlie's busy buying colonies.

ALICE: But not everyone has read her letters. *(holding up a bundle of letters)* I have managed your life for thirty years, so I know where you keep things.

EDWARD tries to snatch the letters.

That's not very gentlemanly. Not the right kind of behaviour for someone who wants to be Master of the King's Musick.

EDWARD: What are you – ?

ALICE: What am I going to do with them? I haven't decided yet. When I found them I wanted to burn them. Either that or burn you. I even wrote to my cousin William to ask his advice on divorce proceedings.

EDWARD: And what did he say? That circumstantial evidence should always be interpreted in the worst possible light?

ALICE: I never posted the note.

EDWARD: Good. Because if you had, you would have looked very foolish.

ALICE: So would you.

EDWARD: Why did you marry me, Alice?

ALICE: Because I fell in love with you.

EDWARD laughs.

I could see your talent, and I knew I was the person to bring it out.

EDWARD: You fell in love with my talent?

ALICE: One has to fall in love with something. A kindly look, a pretty face, a sense of humour. Why not talent?

EDWARD: And you decided my talent would outweigh my social disadvantages?

ALICE: No. As soon as I entered the room and you leapt up from the piano, I simply realised you were the man I wanted to marry.

EDWARD: How?

ALICE: An aura. A radiance.

EDWARD: I was probably sweating.

ALICE: I saw we should have a true understanding.

EDWARD: We do, don't we? After all, I must have fallen in love with you too.

ALICE: No, Eddoo, you were never 'in love' with me. I'm not saying you were a counter-jumper, like my awful aunts who couldn't tell talent from toasted cheese. But I realised ours would be a marriage of minds more than hearts.

EDWARD: Isn't that the best kind of marriage?

ALICE: It certainly requires a bond that grows stronger the more it is tested.

EDWARD: Then ours must be strengthening by the second.

ALICE: Do you still wish you'd married your Helen?

EDWARD: What?

ALICE: You cannot keep secrets like that in a city the size of Worcester.

EDWARD: It wasn't a secret.

ALICE: It was from me.

EDWARD: That's because it was over and done with.

ALICE: I still knew I was second best.

EDWARD: You may have been second, but you were certainly best.

ALICE: But not the love of your life?

EDWARD: I don't know how else to describe you.

ALICE: You just did. Your strength, your staff, your amanuensis. Don't misunderstand me. I know you needed your muses. Your friends if you insist. I soon got over the pain of knowing I wasn't enough. But when you confided in them rather than me, when you stopped asking my opinion, when you refused to share your thoughts about the curious world that goes round and round inside your head, that's when I minded.

EDWARD: Well, I minded that you wouldn't let go.

ALICE: Why should I let go? I was your wife.

EDWARD: That didn't make me your creature.

ALICE: Didn't it? I had to lead you, push you, cajole and comfort you, apologise for you, put up with your moods and your idiocies...

EDWARD: Buy me bigger houses.

ALICE: And why not? Isn't it better than sitting cramped over an upright piano in a parlour no bigger than a coalshed?

EDWARD: Not when it gives me a buzzing in my ears.

ALICE: So I've been wasting my time, have I?

EDWARD: I didn't say that.

ALICE: You're right, Edward. You were not my creature. I was yours. I gave up everything for you. Even my religion.

EDWARD: You'd have made a good vicar's wife, Chicky. Fêtes. Garden parties. Sunday school outings.

ALICE: Are you telling me I needn't have bothered to leave the Church of England and join you and the Irish?

EDWARD: I'm not telling you anything.

ALICE: You never have.

EDWARD: And I never shall, so you may as well rest your voice.

EDWARD begins to beat out a rhythm, but with no melody.

ALICE: What do you believe in, Edward?

EDWARD: Shush.

ALICE: Edward?

EDWARD: The merits of silence.

ALICE: You must believe in something if you want to pluck tunes from the air.

EDWARD: Only that they're there! You see? I've lost it now.

ALICE: Oh. Oh, I'm – [sorry]. There were tears in your eyes when you conducted The Kingdom.

EDWARD: I was weeping for the failure of it.

ALICE: You stood there, beating time with them streaming down your face. *(conducting woodenly)* One-two-three-four, one-two-three-four.

EDWARD: No, no, no, no, no. Not like that. You look like a clockwork parrot.

ALICE: It was in four-four time.

EDWARD: Time? It's not time that matters. It's rhythm.

ALICE: Another subtle difference you've never explained.

EDWARD: Oh, good – [grief] ! All right. Look. Do you see that girl on the swing?

ALICE: What girl?

EDWARD: That girl.

ALICE: Where?

EDWARD: There. It's called imagination, Al. It's what artists have. If you give her a shove, she'll swing faster, and if you don't, she'll run down like a gramophone.

ALICE: She would.

EDWARD: But you won't know which you want until you're standing in front of the band. Sometimes you'll want her to go faster, and sometimes you'll want her to go slower. And sometimes you'll want to put out a hand and stop her altogether, before – letting her go again. You see? Rhythm, not time.

ALICE: Oh.

EDWARD: Rhythm. That's what I believe in. Rhythm. What I've always believed in. Rhythm, notes, music. Not bell, book and Beelzebub.

ALICE: Then why on earth did you write oratorios?

EDWARD: For the same reason I wrote hymn tunes.

ALICE: What?

EDWARD: I'm a lapsed Catholic, all right? I've always had a hankering after the fancy dress.

ALICE: You wrote a hymn to Odin once.

EDWARD: I didn't believe in him either. Writing music is what it says it is, Al. Composing. Putting things together. Things you don't expect to be together.

ALICE: I can understand all that.

EDWARD: Well, that makes a change.

ALICE: Of course I can, because it's like writing a poem.

EDWARD: No!

ALICE: Yes, it is. You have bits of paper pinned up round the room, and I have words pinned up in my head. We are both creating a mosaic.

EDWARD: It's nothing like writing a poem! Words aren't music. Words are just proxies. They stand for things. They're not the things themselves.

ALICE: They are in a poem.

EDWARD: Look at the flowers, Al. What colour's this one? What word describes it?

ALICE: Red.

EDWARD: What sort of red?

ALICE: Rose red.

EDWARD: That's nowhere near it.

ALICE: It is red.

EDWARD: But isn't it more than that? Isn't it much more? *(picking up a record)* Do you remember that thing I used to whistle to tell you I was home?

ALICE: *(singing the four notes: B flat down to G, back up to B flat, and down to A, i.e. the opening note, a note two steps down, a note two steps up, and the note one step down)* Ha-llo I'm home.

EDWARD: No! As soon as you put words to it you make it specific.

ALICE: That's what it meant.

EDWARD: *(putting on the record of the opening of the Enigma Variations)* No, it isn't what it meant. Not when out of it came this.

ALICE: *(over the music)* Six bars in G minor with blank first beats. Then a shift to G major, and descending steps in the last two bars. Then back to G minor and the countermelody.

EDWARD: Yes, all right, all right. That's the programme notes, but when you've said all that, does it tell you what it sounds like?

ALICE: 'Ha-llo I'm home' does.

EDWARD: No, it doesn't. Words are only blunt instruments. But music, when you hear music, when you really hear it with your heart and your soul, it makes your whole body tingle, not just the brain cells you use to work out the price of the groceries. And when it does, it takes your breath away, it strikes you dumb, because it's written on the sky and nothing you can say will do it justice.

He listens for a bit, before stopping the record.

What?

ALICE: I am struck dumb.

EDWARD: Good. Good. In that case, perhaps you'll go back to bed.

ALICE: Perhaps I will.

She starts to move, but stops.

There isn't really an enigma, is there?

EDWARD: Oh, Al!

ALICE: Is there?

EDWARD: Of course there is.

ALICE: What?

EDWARD: You're looking at it.

ALICE: Where?

EDWARD: Here. It's me.

ALICE: *(singing)* Ha-llo it's me.

EDWARD: It's an anagram.

ALICE: Hallo me sit.

EDWARD: What?

ALICE: That's an anagram.

EDWARD: I'm serious, Al. Half-serious.

ALICE: That's a quarter more than usual.

EDWARD: The enigma in the Variations is me.

ALICE: I thought it was a tune.

EDWARD: What tune?

ALICE: The tune that everyone makes such a fuss about. The one that's never played.

EDWARD: I never said it was a tune. The theme that goes through the so-called Enigma Variations and isn't played is me. E in G major. *(speaking the capital letters)* E, I-N, G, M-A.

ALICE: Spelling was never your strongest suit.

EDWARD: I told you. It's an anagram. Good heavens, it's very simple, Al. All you have to do is reverse the I and the N. I'll write it down for you if it helps. E-N-I-G-M-A, Enigma. All right? E, I-N, G, M-A: E in G may. The E is me, E for Elgar...

ALICE: Or Edward.

EDWARD: Or Edward. And as you said yourself, the opening theme begins in G minor, changes to G major – G may – and four bars later it goes back to G minor. And by the time you get to the last Variation, it's pure G major. E is in G may.

ALICE: That's cheating.

EDWARD: Think of it as a question. Am I major or minor?

ALICE: Major, eventually.

EDWARD: You see? You've answered it.

ALICE: So that's all it is? A musical joke?

EDWARD: Not a joke. A riddle.

ALICE: You could have fooled me.

EDWARD: I did.

ALICE: How was I expected to work it out?

EDWARD: If you knew how my mind works it shouldn't have been that hard.

ALICE: Did anyone else guess it was one of your word games?

EDWARD: Only Jaeger.

ALICE: And?

EDWARD: *(meaning Yes)* No, no one else.

ALICE: Then we shall take the secret to the grave.

EDWARD: And our shades will whisper E in G major to each other.

ALICE: Unless Jaeger pushes in between us.

EDWARD: No, he's buried in London, Ducky, and we shall be in Malvern. Unless they scatter me on the Severn.

ALICE: You are not spreading your ashes over half of Worcestershire, Edward. You'll be buried next to me where you belong.

EDWARD: All right, all right. They can scatter my notebooks instead.

ALICE: If you enjoy playing with words, Edward, why are you so dismissive of them?

EDWARD: Words are just fun.

ALICE: And music is serious?

EDWARD: Deadly serious.

ALICE: When we married I thought we should be known for words – your music, of course, but to my poems.

EDWARD: We were. For a while.

ALICE: I remember the first time you refused. You were sitting in the garden in Hereford, doing nothing as usual.

EDWARD: No. I was planning the first symphony.

ALICE: I went down on my knees and offered you a sonnet, and you said no. It made me cry.

EDWARD: I didn't see you.

ALICE: You didn't look.

EDWARD: Al, I'd moved on.

ALICE: And I hadn't?

EDWARD: No.

ALICE: Did I really write that badly?

EDWARD: Abysmally.

ALICE: 'And that is past and that
And what may yet remain?
Dim burning eyes
Slow sobs that rise
No more than that.'

Is that abysmal?

EDWARD: You've had your moments.

ALICE: Alice said I was a poet.

EDWARD: You were a geologist, Chicky. When you looked at the hills you saw rocks, not flowers.

ALICE: I still wanted to write about them.

EDWARD: You still did.

ALICE: What will you write now?

EDWARD: Hm.

ALICE: You ought to finish the opera.

EDWARD shakes his head.

Go back to the piano concerto if you've gone off words. Or another quartet. More of your 'pure' music.

EDWARD: No.

ALICE: The bassoon? You've always wanted to write more for the bassoon.

EDWARD: I've always wanted all kinds of things. A Derby winner. Wolves for the cup. A son-in-law with cash in the bank.

ALICE: What will you write, then?

EDWARD: Nothing.

ALICE: Nothing? What do you mean, nothing?

EDWARD: The negation of thing. A blank. A white sheet of paper.

ALICE: What happened to the notes falling like leaves?

EDWARD: It's going to be a long winter.

ALICE: But you have a gift.

EDWARD: I had a gift.

ALICE: You can't just stop.

EDWARD: Fishing and golf will do from now on.

ALICE: No, they won't.

EDWARD: And perhaps a spot of racing.

ALICE: Edward! Composers don't retire and sit in the rain.

EDWARD: They do when they've run out of tunes.

ALICE: You can't have.

EDWARD: Why do you think I've been combing old notebooks for bell chimes and ten-second polkas?

ALICE: You've always done that.

EDWARD: Which is why I've run out. I might buy a dog again. I could never understand why you hated dogs.

ALICE: Sometimes, Edward, I could shake you.

EDWARD: Shake away, shake away, it won't make any difference. Anyway, golf is good for you. It's good exercise. It's healthier than sitting with your head in your hands. I might go cruising again, if His Majesty's Navy will have me. Welcome aboard, Sir Edward. Stow your tackle in the stateroom and join us for a peg on the poop deck.

ALICE: Edward!

EDWARD: Or more billiards. That's very like golf. *(demonstrating)* You simply read the line, and roll it up.

ALICE: When Alice was here you said music was all around us.

EDWARD: It is.

ALICE: Then why can't you write it down?

EDWARD: Because now when I listen to the wind, I hear the wind. When I look at the trees, I see trees. I no longer hear or see – music.

ALICE: Since when?

EDWARD: Oh, about fifteen years.

ALICE: What!

EDWARD: Give or take. *(still demonstrating billiards)* Now, what about a cannon off the red?

ALICE: What happened?

EDWARD: Hm? Well, it was very odd, really. It was almost as if I went deaf.

ALICE: Like Beethoven?

EDWARD: Oh, when I think of Beethoven I feel like a tinker looking at the Forth Bridge.

ALICE: When was it? No, no, let me guess. It was when you were writing The Kingdom?

EDWARD: It was about then, yes. Have you seen the chalk?

ALICE: Go on.

EDWARD: The Kingdom was a struggle from the start.

ALICE: Even I could see that.

EDWARD: Yes, but once I got into it, the music took me over. Ah, there it is.

ALICE: So you did believe in God?

EDWARD: I wasn't given any choice. I had the words of the Bible hammering in my head, and a voice telling me how to set them. Well, that was all right. I brought on Saint Peter and gave him a sermon.

And that was all right. But then, about half way through, it all stopped. No words, no music. Nothing.

ALICE: But why?

EDWARD: I don't know why!

ALICE: Things like that don't just happen.

EDWARD: It did to me.

ALICE: There must have been some reason.

EDWARD: *(abandoning the billiards)* Ah. Maybe. I don't know.

ALICE: What?

EDWARD: It was just after my father died. In that house in Wales...

ALICE: With the rain pouring down the windows?

EDWARD: Hm? Yes. And I thought back to all those Sundays when I'd been in the organ loft with him. Hearing him cussing and swearing, sneezing from the snuff he kept taking, watching him slip out to the Hop Market during the sermon for a pint, worrying about whether he'd be back in time. And then I looked out of the window at the grey hills and I saw Saint Peter looking back. Dead-eyed. Expressionless. Jangling his keys. I turned to face the wall, hoping he'd go away, but there he was again. And I went down into the deepest, blackest hole I have ever been in.

ALICE: I know. I was standing at the edge.

EDWARD: *(practising an imaginary putting shot)* Now, about ten feet, would you say? Uphill. Coming from the left.

ALICE: Then you went out for a walk?

EDWARD: Hm.

ALICE: And Saint Peter went with you?

EDWARD: Possibly.

ALICE: And the waters of the river had never looked so inviting.

EDWARD: If you know, why are you asking?

ALICE: I reached out my hand, but you wouldn't take it.

EDWARD: I knew it was there. It's what stopped me slipping beneath the surface.

ALICE: What stopped you was my begging the people in Birmingham to accept less than you'd promised.

EDWARD: If you say so. *(the shot)* There you are, you see. Missed!

ALICE: And then?

EDWARD: And then, eventually, when I'd warmed up some old bits of other things and cobbled together a few more words, he picked up the finished score without so much as a by your leave, stuffed it in his music case and bicycled off into the drizzle to moan about me to Mary Magdalene.

ALICE: Bicycled?

EDWARD: He tucked his trousers up first.

ALICE: So it wasn't my awful poems that made you give up words?

EDWARD: Not only, no.

ALICE: Oh, Eddoo, why didn't you tell me?

EDWARD: I couldn't have told you if I'd wanted to. All I knew was that my whole self was falling apart. I remember staring at a painting of Christ in the wilderness, sitting gazing at the ground, trying to understand what life was, what He was, and what death was. And I found myself asking the same questions.

ALICE: If you question everything, you'll end up believing in nothing.

EDWARD: And if you question nothing, you'll end up believing in everything.

ALICE: Isn't that better?

EDWARD: That's why I kept quiet about it. That and the fact that you wouldn't have understood then any more than you do now.

ALICE: Belief is part of life. It's part of being English.

EDWARD: So is doubt.

ALICE: It hurt that you wouldn't talk to me.

EDWARD: It hurt that I couldn't talk to anyone.

ALICE: I still could have helped.

EDWARD: Losing my faith wasn't like losing my hat, you know, Chicky. Oh, hallo, where did I put my faith?

ALICE: What if you hadn't lost it?

EDWARD: My hat or my faith?

ALICE: Either.

EDWARD: You mean God might not have reached down out of the sky and stuffed cotton wool in my ears?

ALICE: If it was God.

EDWARD: I can't think who else it could have been.

ALICE: You might have been punishing yourself.

EDWARD: For writing oratorios to a deity I no longer believed in?

ALICE: Partly.

EDWARD: Or for choosing Alice Stuart as my muse?

ALICE: That as well.

EDWARD: I don't know. All I know is that the brim fell off when I was writing Gerontius, the band went when I was writing The Apostles, and you were right – the crown was blown away by The Kingdom.

ALICE: And now?

EDWARD: Now I'm bunkered. Bunkered at the diminished seventh. Hatless in the blazing sun.

ALICE: I'm sorry.

EDWARD: Sorry? You're sorry?

ALICE: Yes.

EDWARD: I'm sorry. Played three. Won one, drawn one, lost one. Not a brilliant record, even for a provincial. Especially when I shall be best remembered for Land of Old and Poorly.

ALICE: No, Eddoo. You'll be remembered for the rhythms of the land and the wind in the trees.

EDWARD: Only by the trees.

ALICE: And the reeds by the Severn and the Teme.

EDWARD: I'll take my stick to them if they forget.

ALICE: And what shall I be remembered for?

EDWARD: You won't be. Unless I am.

ALICE: Then we shall both die miserable.

EDWARD: And what happens in the meantime, before that blessed reunion?

ALICE: You'd better ask your muse.

EDWARD: Hallo, Muse. Can you toss me down another string quartet? See? Not a quaver.

ALICE: Eddoo, did you ever truly love me?

EDWARD: I did. Yes. Did you truly love me?

ALICE: Yes, my little Doo-doo.

EDWARD: Despite my moods, my idiocies and my muses?

ALICE: Yes, Eddoo. Oh, yes.

EDWARD: It's not been so terrible, has it?

ALICE: Not a bit.

EDWARD: We were happy enough sometimes.

ALICE: In Garmisch, listening to the oompah band.

EDWARD: And Capri, picking olives.

ALICE: Except on the ferry.

EDWARD: You can be seasick in the bath.

ALICE: Peasants in garlic, you called them.

EDWARD: They were pickled in cider, in Hereford. Do you remember when they asked me to be mayor?

ALICE: I could never think why.

EDWARD: I declare the ears of this city – finally open!

ALICE: You will go back home to the apples and pears when I'm dead, won't you?

EDWARD: To the stuffiest fruits on God's good earth?

ALICE: They're the heart of England, Eddoo.

EDWARD: And to stir them up, I shall don academic dress and conduct Gerontius in every cathedral in the west of England.

ALICE: Will you really never compose another Gerontius?

EDWARD: Not now I'm one myself. A grumpy, worn-out old sinner.

ALICE: Not even for my sake?

EDWARD: I can't, my little wopsicle.

ALICE: Not without the gift of plucking tunes out of the air?

EDWARD: Not without you.

ALICE: To rule your staves for you?

EDWARD: More than that.

ALICE: To fend off your visitors? To manage your diary?

EDWARD: To tell me that you believe in me.

ALICE: Can't your friends do that?

EDWARD: What friends?

ALICE: Edward.

EDWARD: You were my friend. Everyone else was an acquaintance.

ALICE: Even Ivory Hatpins?

EDWARD: Even him.

ALICE: And Alice Stuart Wortley?

EDWARD slowly shakes his head.

Are all creative artists so lonely?

EDWARD: Probably. But we're too withdrawn to find out.

ALICE: Is that why you hid in Birchwood and Brinkwells?

EDWARD: It's why I hid among the test tubes.

ALICE: Why you made awful jokes?

EDWARD: M-hm.

ALICE: Oh, Eddoo, I wish I had been beautiful for you.

EDWARD: You were. You are.

ALICE: Tell me I'm your ickle Chickabiddy.

EDWARD: Oo knows oo is, Chickabiddy.

ALICE: *(singing 'In Haven', Sea Pictures No. 2)*
'Closely let me hold thy hand,
Storms are sweeping sea and land;
Love alone will stand.'

EDWARD: *(joining in)*
'Kiss my lips, and softly say:
"Joy, sea-swept, may fade today;
Love alone will stay."'

ALICE: Come to bed soon, my darling Zoo-zoo.

EDWARD: I shall, I shall. But I must just write down this tune that's come back into my head.

ALICE: From where?

EDWARD: From whoever it is that hangs them on the clouds.

ALICE: Is it a funeral march for me?

EDWARD: No, no, it's a quick march. To keep you very much alive.

ALICE goes back to the bed. EDWARD hums the forceful rhythm.

But there's no melody. It's only drums. Drums without fifes. Or is it the beating of my heart?

SARAH comes in, sees ALICE stirring and turns to EDWARD.

SARAH: Sir, I think you'd better come. Lady Alice is awake.

EDWARD: I know.

SARAH: Do you?

EDWARD: Yes. I know.

SARAH: But...

EDWARD: We've been talking to each other...

SARAH: *(to herself)* I see.

SARAH goes off.

EDWARD: *(overlapping, going to the bed)* ...haven't we, Chicky? We've been saying things we should have said years ago.

ALICE chokes.

Come on, don't leave me now. Not now, Ducky. Not now. I'll write the opera. I'll set the rest of your songs. Only don't go now. Don't go, my little rabbit. Not now. Oo's not going to leave me nowdeday, my Chickabiddy. Oo can't leave me now. Not now. Not –

ALICE dies in EDWARD's arms.

SARAH comes in.

SARAH: Sir? It's Lady Stuart of Wortley.

EDWARD: Hm?

SARAH: Lady Alice Stuart Wortley. On the telephone.

EDWARD: Would you tell her that I can't leave my wife.

SARAH goes off.

Because we still have so much to say.

Oh Alice. Alice.

Elgar's Salut d'amour plays, becoming louder.

END